50 Empowering Poems
to Ignite Your Child's Potential

Unleashing Greatness: 50 Empowering Poems to Ignite Your Child's Potential

For information about this title or to order other books and/or electronic media, contact the publisher, Euodoo Transformational Coaching, at euodootransformationalcoaching@gmail.com

Euodoo Transformational Coaching

ISBNs:
979-8-9922306-0-4 (softcover)
979-8-9922306-1-1 (eBook)

Printed in the United States of America

Cover and Interior Design: 1106 Design

Dedication

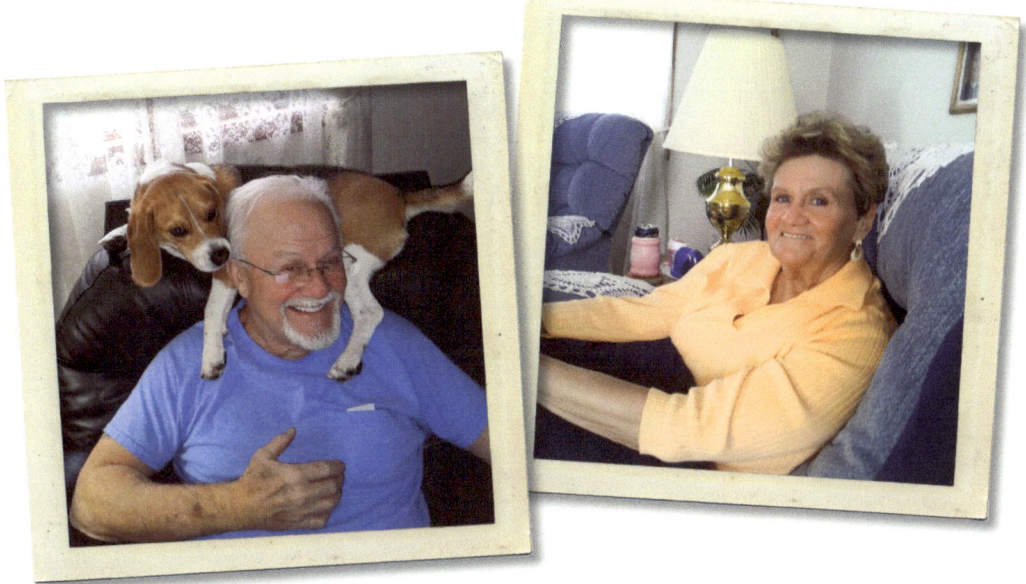

This book is dedicated to Donna, my wife of 57 years, who is extremely patient, forgiving, and thoughtful; to Buddy (our Beagle), who constantly reminds me that he wants more play time and more dog treats; to my children, Kristy, Jeannie, and Brian; to my sister Sharon; and to all my friends and other family members for their support and encouragement.

I love and appreciate you all.

"Reading to your child, even for only a few minutes each day, can literally change their world."

—David W. Waugh

Introduction

Even though you are a good parent, grandparent, or guardian, are you doing enough to ensure that your children will experience a future filled with happiness and abundance? This book may be your tool for helping them avoid unnecessary hardships in their future and propel them toward a life filled with happiness and success.

This book is a collection of fifty poems that can enrich the lives of your children and forever mold their character. By reading and discussing these life-altering poems daily with your children, you can help them avoid some of life's ugliest snares that entrap so many of our youths. You could skyrocket your children's success in creating strong, loving relationships with family and friends, in succeeding in school and extracurricular activities, and in establishing a foundation for a more abundant future.

Many of these poems, with their corresponding questions, are interconnected and overlapping, thus serving as a reinforcement of the principles being presented. Reading and discussing as little as one poem a day over a period of several years could benefit your children throughout their entire lives. It could change their world.

It's been postulated that your outside world is a direct reflection of your inner world. Plainly speaking, your innermost beliefs and thoughts, which create your responses to the world around you, will directly influence what happens in your life. Therefore, to change your world, you must simply change your inner beliefs and thoughts. It's as simple as that. With this book, you could begin changing your children's world one poem at a time.

So, what is in your children's future? Will it be hopelessness and hardship, or will it be joy and abundance? You can make the difference. You can influence the outcome.

Preface

For the last twelve years of my career, I've had the privilege of collaborating with a publisher of children's books. I have traveled extensively and met people from all levels of society (legislators, law enforcement, school administrators, teachers, doctors, lawyers, corporate executives, franchise owners, plumbers, carpenters, electricians, factory employees, and others).

During my travels, I became increasingly aware of a significant divide between children and many adults. Allow me to explain. Have you ever noticed the openness and free spirit that young children display? They express love, curiosity, excitement, enthusiasm, and an entire range of emotions. They love life. It's exciting for them. They bounce around with all sorts of energy while laughing, playing, and enjoying each other's companionship. If you just watch and listen to them on any playground, you can see their energy and sense their excitement—as though every day holds something new and exciting for them.

What is happening to many of these children when they grow up? Why have so many of them lost their zest and excitement for living? Why do many of them struggle with relationships? Why do they change jobs often, and why do they often fail at business? Why do many of them turn to alcohol and drugs?

Personally, I have met with many of these people throughout my life, and it's truly a tragedy. As we all know, life can be a struggle, with its repeated disappointments. Life can wear a person down and lead them astray. It can be relentless and cruel if one isn't adequately prepared both mentally and emotionally for its difficulties.

From my experience and observations, I believe that the reason so many of these people are living an unfulfilling life is their inability to interact successfully in their social environment, their lack of belief in themselves, their lack of faith in their future, and their lack of the skills to improve their lives.

Here is just one of those observations. I've noticed far too many adults have difficulty with carrying on a simple conversation with someone they've just met. In severe cases, they may shun all interactions with people they don't know. A simple "Good morning" on the street to a passing stranger can be a challenge for many of them. I have noticed that this withdrawal and lack of interaction seem to be getting increasingly worse over time. More people are distancing themselves from one another. Many of them have withdrawn into themselves or surrounded themselves with those with similar personalities.

Little do these people realize that there are fundamental skills to creating a full and abundant life. Without these skills, achieving any level of success in life, no matter how you describe "success," would be extremely difficult, if not impossible. There is absolutely no reason these people should suffer throughout their young-adult years. They can be taught these skills early in life.

Are you aware that personal development for adults has become an enormous industry over the last hundred years or so? Today, one can find multiple avenues to develop personal skills—by attending seminars, studying online courses, watching online videos, reading blogs, listening to or watching podcasts online or streaming, and reading books. Over several decades, I have read dozens of these books, by some of the world's most renowned authors (e.g., Napoleon Hill, Jim Rohn, Anthony Robbins, Zig Ziglar, Robert Schuller, John C. Maxwell, Les Brown, Tom Hopkins, Jack Canfield, Dale Carnegie, Maxwell Maltz, Brian Tracy, and many more), and, as a result, I have been blessed with a very successful sales career and earned more than a dozen production awards.

Why can't these principles be taught to our children while they are still young, impressionable, and eager to learn? Why must they wait until they become adults? This is the reason I have authored this book of poems.

This book can give your children a much greater chance for a bright and successful future. If read and discussed with your children on a regular schedule, it can minimize the struggles that lie ahead for them by teaching them the personal skills, social skills, and success principles necessary to strengthen their character and their ability to interact more effectively with their peers.

These poems are intended to be only conversation starters. More important are the discussions that follow each poem. Suggested questions have been provided to stimulate your discussion. When you discuss these poems with your children, you will be reinforcing the concepts and principles in the poems.

It's never too early or too late for you to start reading and discussing these poems with your children. Won't you help them grow up to be mentally and emotionally strong, personable, and ready to tackle the world with enthusiasm and belief in themselves? Your decision will most assuredly have a direct bearing on their future.

Table of Contents

1. Let's Read Some Poems

As I read you these poems one at a time,
you must listen to them. They can strengthen your mind.
So, pay attention, and lend an ear,
to some important ideas you're about to hear.

Engaging Questions to Ask Your Child

▸ I like *learning*, and I like *poems*. Both can be fun! Are you ready now to have some fun and learn some new things?
▸ What would you like to learn more about?
▸ Learning makes you smart. What do you think will happen when you get smarter?
▸ Let's pay close attention to what I am about to read to you, and both of us will get smarter, okay?

 2. Listening

Do you know that I want the best for you?
You should listen to me whatever you do!
I know what's right and what's wrong, you see.
So, be a good listener. Don't you agree?
When friends want to talk, you should listen to them.
Never interrupt—after all, you're their friend.
Being a good listener should be important to you,
because *learning comes from listening*,
and that's what you should do.
Learning is important, as you will soon see.
You will learn so much more by listening to me.
So, listen with care as I read to you.
Listen and learn, and become smarter, too.

Engaging Questions to Ask Your Child

- ▶ Do you know that I love you and want you to grow up knowing the difference between right and wrong?
- ▶ When you don't know if something is right or wrong, will you please ask me?
- ▶ So, *listen* very closely to me. Okay?
- ▶ When was the last time you didn't know if something was right or wrong?
- ▶ Do you understand why interrupting someone when they are speaking is not polite?
- ▶ Does it bother you when someone interrupts while you're speaking?
- ▶ *Listening more than talking* will make you a whole lot smarter. Always pay close attention when someone is speaking to you. Okay?
- ▶ You want to get smarter, don't you?

 3. Learning

Learning is important. It's important to do.
It's important to me. It's important to you.
Learning is something we should do every day.
So, let's keep learning. What do you say?
Every day, we should learn something new.
I've learned something today. How about you?

Engaging Questions to Ask Your Child

▸ What have we learned so far today?
▸ Is there anything that you want to *learn* more about?
▸ I am curious, and I always like to learn new things. How about you? Are you curious?
▸ Smart people are curious about things. Do you want to get smart?
▸ Let's both try to learn something today and every day. Okay?
▸ Do you think that we will learn more and get smarter by reading these poems?

4. Reading

(If Your Child Reads)

Reading can make you smart, you know.
Reading a lot will help your mind grow.
The more you read, the smarter you'll be.
So, pick up that book, and read it to me.
If there is a word that you really don't know,
then ask me to explain it, and I will do so.
When you read a lot, you will learn many things,
like why dogs bark and why birds sing.
Let's start to *read* and to *learn every day*,
and we'll have some fun along the way.

Engaging Questions to Ask Your Child

▸ Do you like to *read*?
▸ What do you like to read about?
▸ Do you understand that reading every day will make you smarter about a lot of stuff?
▸ You want to get smarter, don't you?

4. Reading (cont.)

(If Your Child Doesn't Read)

Reading can make you smart, you know.
Reading a lot will help your mind grow.
The more I read to you, the smarter you'll be.
Listen as I read, and pay close attention to me.
If there is a word that you really don't know,
then ask me to explain it, and I will do so.
When you learn to read, you will learn many things,
like why dogs bark and why birds sing.
Let's start to *read* and to *learn every day*.
Let's have some fun. What do you say?

Engaging Questions to Ask Your Child

▶ Would you like me to read more to you? (or) Would you like me to help you *learn to read*?
▶ Did you know that reading every day will make us smarter about a lot of stuff?
▶ You want us to get smarter, don't you?
▶ What kind of things do you want me to read about?

5. Liking Yourself

When you look into the mirror, what do you see?
A smile on your face is what it should be!
Now take a deep breath, and look all around.
There's no one like you. They'll never be found.
Because you are different—and that's a good thing.
Being special to the world is what you bring.
So, let your light shine wherever you go,
and be that bright candle with your warmth and your glow.
Never let anyone change who you are,
because you are a bright and shining star.
Try looking and smiling into the mirror every day.
Then happiness should follow you along your way.

Engaging Questions to Ask Your Child

▸ Do you *like yourself*?
▸ What do you like about yourself?
▸ Do you know why it is important to like yourself and to like who you are?
▸ Do you know that when you like yourself, you will be happier, and when you are happier, more people will like you? People like happy people.
▸ Do you know that when you like yourself, you will smile a lot more?
▸ Have you ever noticed that when you smile, almost everyone smiles back? Smiling makes other people feel happier. That's why they smile back.
▸ Try looking into the mirror every day and saying, *"I like you"* to yourself. All right? It will make you much happier.
▸ Do you know that you are special? Let's talk about that. Okay?

6. Believing in Yourself

Believing in yourself and what you can do
should be one of the most important things to you.
When you believe in yourself and improve every day,
there are very few things that can stand in your way.
It becomes easier to get things done,
and believing in yourself makes doing them fun.
So, believe in yourself and what you can do.
Believe in yourself and you'll see that it's true.

Engaging Questions to Ask Your Child

▸ Do you know what it means to *believe in yourself*? What do you think it means? Do you want me to explain?
▸ Do you know what it means to *have confidence*? I can explain it for you.
▸ Do you know that I believe in you and have confidence in you because I know you are smart and that you are happy? I also know that you will grow up to be one of those exceptionally good people who love and respect themselves and others!
▸ Now, do you believe in yourself?
▸ Do you know that when you believe in yourself, you can get more things done—and that it can be fun, too?

7. Daily Self-Talk/Affirmations

Talking to yourself is not always wrong.
If your talk is encouraging, it can make you strong.
Tell yourself things like, "I will always be nice."
"Before I say anything, I will think twice."
"Every day, I will do my best in school."
"I am doing my best to follow that rule."
"I am feeling happy and joyful today,
and that is the way I am going to stay."
"I'm feeling healthy and strong,
and I'm going to feel this way all day long."

Engaging Questions to Ask Your Child

▸ Do you *talk to yourself*—either silently or out loud?
▸ If you talk to yourself, what do you say?
▸ Do you tell yourself things that will make you a stronger, smarter, and better person in every way?
▸ How would you like to grow stronger, smarter, and better?
▸ (If Your Child Reads) Do you want me to help you make a list of things to say to yourself every day? We can make a little book to put them in, and we will keep that book in your room. We'll call your book the "I AM" book. You can read your "I AM" book every day when you first wake up. We can put things in it like, "I am a Grade-A student" or "I am getting smarter every day." We can put in something like "I am a polite and caring person." (Statements like this are called "Affirmations.") What things do you think we should put in your "I AM" book?
▸ (If Your Child Doesn't Read) Do you want me to help you make a list of things to say to yourself every day? We can make a little book to put them in, and we will keep that book in your room. We'll call your book the "I AM" book. I can read your "I AM" book to you every day when you first wake up. You can repeat the things with me as I read them to you. We can put things in it like "I am a Grade-A student" or "I am getting smarter every day." We can put in something like "I am a polite and caring person." (Statements like this are called "Affirmations.") What things do you think we should put in your "I AM" book"? When you get older, you can read them to yourself every day.

8. Thinking Happy Thoughts

Did you know that changing your thoughts to what's happy and good,
can change your world? It most certainly could.
Changing your thoughts and putting a smile on your face
will make your world a happier place.
To change your world, you must change within.
So, change your thoughts, and maintain that grin.
Just look inside, and you will find
you have what it takes—an intelligent mind.

Engaging Questions to Ask Your Child

► Do you know that thinking bad thoughts can make you sad, unhappy, or even angry sometimes?
► Have you ever had bad thoughts? What were they?
► Do you know that you can change sadness to happiness if you think really hard about the things that make you happy? So, when you're unhappy, just try changing your thoughts to what makes you happy and what makes you smile.
► Do you know that people will like you when you smile?
► Will you try to *stay happy* as much as you can?
► What are some of your *happy thoughts*?

9. Making Every Day a Great Day

Every morning when you get out of bed,
get really excited about your day ahead.
Think of things that are exciting to you,
and keep that excitement the entire day through.
Smile and be happy as you go through the day.
Share your excitement with those along your way.

Engaging Questions to Ask Your Child

- ▶ Do you get out of bed excited and look forward to your day ahead?
- ▶ Do you know that you can decide each day to be happy and excited? It's a choice you make.
- ▶ Will you try to *be happy every day*? Keep those happy thoughts in your head all day long. Think of things that make you happy.
- ▶ What thoughts make you feel happy?
- ▶ Do you know that most people you meet will smile back at you if you smile at them first? That's a good way to stay happy, isn't it? Go through each day giving everyone a great big smile.

10. Love

Love is a feeling deep from within.
Straight from your heart is where it begins.
Love is gentle, and love is kind.
Love is patient all the time.
Love is forgiving and compassionate as well.
And I love you . . . can't you tell? *(while squeezing your child)*

Engaging Questions to Ask Your Child

▸ What do you think *love* is? Can you tell me? Let me give you some examples: *love of pets, love of family, love of friends,* and so on.
▸ Where does your love come from?
▸ Who do you love—and why?
▸ You know that I love you a whole bunch, right? I love you to the moon and back! *(while squeezing your child again)*

11. Doing What's Right

Doing what's right should always be done.
Sometimes it's hard. Sometimes it's fun.
If you are confused and don't know what to do,
you can ask me, and I will help you.
I want you to know what's right and what's wrong.
I will carefully teach you. It shouldn't take long.
I love you and care for you more than you know,
and my love and respect for you is what I will show.

Engaging Questions to Ask Your Child

- Do you get confused sometimes about *what's right and what's wrong*?
- When was the last time you were confused? Tell me about it.
- Will you always ask me if you don't know?
- Do you understand that I love you and that I want you to grow up knowing the difference between right and wrong?
- Will you try to understand that I want the best for you and will do everything I can to help you?

12. Being Dependable

If you were asked to do something today,
would you say to yourself, "I would rather go play"?
When you are dependable, people rely upon you
to do those things that they asked you to do.
Being dependable is being responsible as well.
When you are responsible, people can tell.
Being dependable is a wonderful way to be.
People will respect you. Just wait and see.

Engaging Questions to Ask Your Child

- ▶ Do you understand what *being dependable* means?
- ▶ Would you like me to give you some examples?
- ▶ Do you believe you are dependable? Can you give me some examples of what being dependable means?
- ▶ When you are dependable, people will respect you more.
- ▶ Do you understand what respect is? Respect is treating others with kindness—treating them the way you want to be treated. It will be explained more in poem number 14, "Respecting Other People."
- ▶ Do you want other people to respect you? Do you want me to respect you?
- ▶ Do you want me to explain why respect is important?
- ▶ Let's go to the next poem, "Being Responsible." Okay? It will help you understand more about being dependable.

13. Being Responsible

Do you have a pet? Like a fish, cat, or dog?
Or maybe you have a little green frog.
It doesn't matter what pets are in your home;
you should love and care for them, and make them your own.
Taking care of your pets can be a big chore.
You must feed them and train them—and a whole lot more.
Being responsible means that you must care,
because they depend on you for their welfare.
Being responsible is something all of us need.
Being responsible is most important, indeed.
Can you think of something you are responsible for?
Think really hard. There's probably more.

Engaging Questions to Ask Your Child

▶ Do you understand what *being responsible* means? Let me give you some examples: *keeping your room clean, picking up your toys, putting up your bike, brushing your teeth,* and so on.

▶ If I get you a pet, would you be responsible enough to take care of it? *(optional)*

▶ Can you tell me some of the things you are responsible for?

▶ Do you understand the importance of being responsible? Do you want me to explain it some more?

14. Respecting Other People

Respect for others is a good trait.
Respecting others could determine everyone's fate.
If you treat others with meanness, then they become sad.
Sadness is terrible. Sadness is bad.
So, treat others with kindness, whatever they do.
Be a good person, through and through.
By respecting others in things big and small,
you can bring joy and happiness to all.

Engaging Questions to Ask Your Child

▶ What does respect mean to you? Do you understand it? Do you want me to explain it some more?
▶ Do you respect me?
▶ Who else do you respect?
▶ Do you understand that you must first show *respect for others* before they can respect you?

15. Lifting Up Others

Always be happy for other people's success.
Congratulate them, and wish them the best.
Lifting up others is what you should do.
Lifting up others can be fun, too.
When you lift up others, you should feel warm inside,
for making them happy or knowing you tried.
When you treat others like you want them to treat you,
you'll be rewarded with many friends, too.

Engaging Questions to Ask Your Child

▶ *Lifting up* other people—*encouraging them* and *reminding them of their best qualities*—makes them feel good. Does lifting up other people make *you* feel good, too? It does me.
▶ Have you ever made someone feel good? Tell me about it.
▶ Do you know that, when you make others feel good, it will help you to make more friends?
▶ Do you want more friends? Who else would you like to be friends with?
▶ Do you know that you should treat others like you want them to treat you?

16. Respecting Others' Opinions

Sometimes your friends will believe differently than you,
and that's okay—they have the right to.
Respect their opinions. You may believe they are wrong.
But don't argue with them. You need to stay strong.
Stay firm in your beliefs, and do what is right.
Treat them with kindness, with all of your might.
Your beliefs and your values are important to you.
Stay strong in them, whatever you do.

Engaging Questions to Ask Your Child

▶ Do you understand what *respecting others' opinions* means?
▶ If someone doesn't agree with you, do you get upset? You shouldn't. They have a right to disagree and have their own opinion.
▶ If you disagree with someone, disagree politely. Okay?
▶ Have you ever disagreed with someone? Tell me about it.
▶ What will you do the next time someone disagrees with you?
▶ Do you understand that many people may believe differently than you?
▶ Do you know that it's all right to have an opinion that's different from someone else's?

 17. Never Arguing

Try not to argue. It's not a good thing.
Pain and suffering are all that it brings.
You can lose friends and many others, too.
So, arguing isn't a good thing to do.
When you disagree, it's okay to say,
"I disagree"—and leave it that way.
If you want to explain your point of view,
do it with understanding—and kindness, too.

Engaging Questions to Ask Your Child

▶ Do you know that no one wins an argument?

▶ Arguing just creates anger and bad feelings, right?

▶ Have you ever argued with anyone? What was it about? How did that end?

▶ What does *being disrespectful* mean to you? Do you want me to explain it?

▶ Do you understand that *arguing is disrespectful*? Everyone deserves an opinion, even if it is different from yours.

▶ Did you know that arguing can cause you to lose friends? Have you ever lost a friend because of arguing?

18. Giving and Receiving

If you want good things to come your way,
be of good cheer—it could happen one day.
Giving what you want is the first thing to do.
Then wait for the same to come back to you.
If it's love that you want, then it's love you should give.
It will be love you'll receive in this life that you live.
If it's friendship that you want, then it's friendship you must show.
Have the faith that your friendships will grow.
Never forget that, *to receive, you must first give.*
Then, see what a wonderful life you'll live.

Engaging Questions to Ask Your Child

▸ Do you like giving things to others? I enjoy giving to others. It makes me feel good.
▸ Do you like to feel good?
▸ Do you like receiving things from family and friends?
▸ Which do you like best—giving or receiving?
▸ Giving can be fun, and it makes you feel good. When you give someone something, does it make you feel good? Tell me about it.
▸ *Do you know that, the more you give, the more you will receive?*
▸ Do you understand what it means to be *generous*?
▸ Are you generous? Give me some examples of your generosity.
▸ Do you understand why you must give first before receiving? *You must first **give** love, friendship, and respect before you can **receive** them.*

19. Sharing

If you had some ice cream, and a friend came by,
would you share it with them, or would you make them cry?
Not sharing is *stingy.* It's mean, and it's cruel.
But you're not that way, because you know this rule:
That "sharing is caring," and to share is good.
You know how to share,
and you know that you should.

Engaging Questions to Ask Your Child

- Do you like to *share* things? You can share your time, your toys, a book, your ice cream, or candy . . . all kinds of things!
- What things have you shared with others? Tell me.
- Do you know that when you share, it makes you feel good inside? How does it make you feel inside when you share something?
- Do you want to feel good inside?
- When you share, do you want those with whom you share to feel good, too?
- It should be important to you to make other people feel good! Right?

20. Helping Others

If a friend were to say, "Can you help me today?"
you should show them that you care.
You should help them out in every way
and let them know you'll be there.
You never know when *you'll* need some help.
Being kind and thoughtful is good.
Your friends will remember when you helped them out
and will offer to help you . . . understood?

Engaging Questions to Ask Your Child

▶ Do you know that, when you help others, they will more than likely help you when you need it? I enjoy *helping others*. I am helping us both right now by reading to you and making both of us smarter.

▶ Tell me about the last time you helped someone.

▶ How does helping someone make you feel? Does it make you feel good?

▶ It's important to help others feel good, too. Right?

21. Never Gossip or Lie

Never talk badly about someone else.
Those kinds of thoughts should be kept to yourself.
You wouldn't want someone to say bad things about you.
So, putting down others is a terrible thing to do.
You know that a lie is something that's untrue.
Has someone passed a lie on to you?
If you repeat it, that would be wrong;
you could lose friends, and that wouldn't take long.
So, always be truthful in all that you say.
Don't gossip or lie. You'll be happier that way.

Engaging Questions to Ask Your Child

▶ Do you know what *gossiping* means? It means *putting someone down* or *talking badly about them behind their back*—and it is wrong. It is disrespectful and bad.

▶ Has anyone ever gossiped to you about someone else? What did you do?

▶ Have you ever gossiped about someone else? How did that turn out?

▶ Do you understand that *lying* is harmful and hurtful? Never tell a lie! You can lose friends, and you would disappoint me!

22. Being Truthful

Lying isn't nice to do,
and people could lose their trust in you.
Just tell the truth, and you will see
how much better you feel around others (and me).
When a lie is found out, others get sad.
They'll know you lied; some will even get mad.
So, never tell a lie at all.
Then you won't have to worry. You can stand tall.

Engaging Questions to Ask Your Child

▶ Lying is bad—it is the opposite of *being truthful*. It can hurt someone. Do you want me to explain, or do you understand?

▶ Do you know that people can lose their respect for you when they catch you in a lie? That hurts you, right? So, never tell a lie! *Always be truthful!* All right?

23. Being Thankful

Be thankful for your blessings every day.
Be thankful for good things that come your way.
Be thankful for your family who loves you.
Be thankful for all your friends, too.
Be thankful for what you have learned from me.
Be thankful for how smart you'll be.
Be thankful for things as much as you can,
and, one day, you may just understand.
You will be blessed in more ways than one
and will attract things that make your life fun.

Engaging Questions to Ask Your Child

▸ Do you know what *being thankful* means?

▸ What things are you thankful for?

▸ I am thankful for you. Are you thankful for me?

▸ Being thankful for many things makes me feel good inside. What about you?

▸ Do you know that being thankful will make you feel happier? When you are happier, it makes others around you feel happier! Being thankful makes you feel good inside!

▸ Being thankful as much as you can attracts many good things into your life. Did you know that? It can affect your whole life.

▸ *(If Your Child Reads)* Would you like me to make a Gratitude Book, where we can list all the things you are thankful for? Do you understand what *gratitude* means? If you want, we can make that book and put it in your room. You can read them and add to them every day. What sort of things are you grateful for that we can write in your Gratitude Book?

▸ *(If Your Child Doesn't Read)* Would you like me to make a Gratitude Book, where we can list all the things you are thankful for? If you don't understand *gratitude*, I can explain it. If you want, we can make that book and put it in your room. I can read them to you every day. As I read each of them to you, you can repeat them back to me. All right? We can even add to them whenever you want. When you get older, you can read them to yourself every day. What sort of things are you grateful for that we can write in your Gratitude Book?

24. Being Humble

Always remember that life isn't just about you.
You are important, but so are others, too.
Stay modest and humble in everything you say and do,
and many others will be attracted to you.
Show kindness and caring as you go through each day,
and most people will treat you in the same way.

Engaging Questions to Ask Your Child

▶ Do you know what *modest* and *humble* mean? Let me explain. It means *not feeling or acting like you are better than others.*

▶ Do you know that *being modest and humble* helps you to feel good inside? You want to feel good inside, don't you?

▶ Do you know how to be modest and humble?

▶ Have you ever been modest or humble? When? Tell me about it.

▶ Are you kind to others? Tell me more.

▶ Do you remember that you should treat others like you want them to treat you? Then everyone will feel better.

25. Dreaming

Dreams don't come true overnight.
If they are worth it, you must fight.
Fight to make your dreams come true,
and they may happen just for you.
Some dreams don't come easy, but that's okay.
You know how to stick. You know how to stay.
So, don't give up. Stand your ground.
Those dreams you chase will come around.

Engaging Questions to Ask Your Child

▸ Do you know what I mean by a *dream*? A *dream* is *a thought that you wish would come true.*

▸ Do you have anything you wish to come true? When you grow up, would you like to become a doctor, a chef, a firefighter, a nurse?

▸ Where would you like to go? Where would you like to visit?

▸ Goals help you make your dreams come true. I will explain goals in the next poem, "Setting Goals."

▸ Goals can help you never give up on living your dreams. Did you know that?

▸ Did you know that dreaming and goal-setting go together? They help to keep your dreams alive and exciting.

26. Setting Goals

Have you set a goal today?
"What's a goal?" you may say.
A goal is something you want to get done.
And writing them down can be lots of fun.
A goal can be many things, too.
Like reading a book or going to the zoo.
You can trust me, because I know
that setting goals will help you grow!
So, set a goal every day,
and watch what happens. What do you say?

Engaging Questions to Ask Your Child

▶ Do you understand what a *goal* is? Let me explain. A goal can be *a dream or a wish that you want to come true.*

▶ Do you want to know one of my goals? One of my goals is to help you grow up and have an incredibly happy and fun life.

▶ Did you know there are daily goals and long-term goals?

▶ Would you like to know what some of my daily goals are?

▶ Would you like to know what some of my long-term goals are?

▶ Would you like me to help you *set some daily goals*? We can write them down.

▶ Do you want me to help you write down some long-term goals?

▶ *(If Your Child Reads)* Would you like us to make a nice Goal Board to put in your room? We can post all your goals on that board, where you can read them every day! What are some goals that you would like to put on your Goal Board?

▶ *(If Your Child Doesn't Read)* Would you like us to make a nice Goal Board to put in your room? We can post all your goals on that board, and I can read them to you every day! You can repeat them back to me as I read them to you. When you get older, you can read them to yourself every day. What are some goals that you would like to put on your Goal Board?

27. Don't Be a Quitter

Always give the best you can.
Never quit. Make a stand.
If quitting should ever cross your mind,
Always remember the following line:
"True winners never quit, and quitters never win."
So, stand your ground. Never think of quitting again.

Engaging Questions to Ask Your Child

- You're not a *quitter*, are you?
- Have you ever quit trying? Tell me about it.
- Do you know that for a dream or wish to come true, you must never quit trying to achieve it? That is why you should always have a goal and look at that Goal Board in your room every day.
- Do you know that you can never win at anything if you continue to quit? Quitting can become a habit—and that isn't good.

28. Being Unstoppable

When you're doing something that's important to you,
like cleaning your room or finishing homework that's due.
Never let anything get in your way.
Work till it's finished. Then you can play.
Being unstoppable is being real smart.
Make it a habit to finish what you start.
When you become unstoppable, people will say,
"Now there is a person who'll be successful someday."

Engaging Questions to Ask Your Child

▶ Do you understand what *being unstoppable* means? Can you explain it to me? *Being unstoppable* means that *you must stay determined to finish whatever you start.*

▶ Do you want to be a winner and unstoppable? Remember that you are not a quitter. Right?

▶ Do you understand that, when you develop the habit of being unstoppable, you can accomplish many things? That is a wonderful habit.

29. Staying Motivated

If there is something you want to do,
then staying motivated is important for you.
Create a picture of that thing in your mind.
Stay excited and enthusiastic all the time.
That picture in your mind of what you want to do
can motivate you to make it come true.

Engaging Questions to Ask Your Child

- Do you understand what *staying motivated* means? It means *holding onto your enthusiasm and your desire for achieving something*. Enthusiasm and excitement will help drive you forward. Do you understand?
- Let me give you an example, okay? Have you ever been excited about going to a school play or going on a vacation? Do you remember how excited you were about going? Well, that was being motivated. Does that help you to understand better?
- Tell me about when you were excited and motivated about something.
- Staying motivated helps you achieve more. Staying motivated can make things easier and more fun to accomplish. You can even get things done faster when you are motivated. Did you know that?

30. Doing Your Best

You should do your best at whatever you do,
because you have the talent deep within you.
Never let anything stand in your way,
and you will be happy at what most people say.
They will say that you are determined to do your best,
and you'll probably achieve a great deal of success.

Engaging Questions to Ask Your Child

- ▶ Do you understand why *doing your best* is important?
- ▶ Do you understand that you are special and that you have a lot of talent within you? You will acquire even more talent as you grow older. But you must listen closely as I read these poems. Okay?
- ▶ Does doing your best make you feel good about yourself? It should.
- ▶ Doing your best is an excellent quality to have. It will benefit you all your life. Okay?
- ▶ People respect those who do their best. Do you know that?
- ▶ Do you try to always do your best at whatever you are doing? When have you tried doing your best recently?

31. Seeing Yourself as a Winner

If being a winner is important to you,
then there are a few things you must learn to do.
Start by imagining and seeing yourself win.
Form a vision in your mind, deep down within.
Hold onto that vision, and believe it'll come true,
and you may see it happen someday for you.

Engaging Questions to ask Your Child

▶ Is *being a winner* something that interests you?

▶ Have you ever heard of visualization? It's a trick that a lot of winners use. Athletes use it a lot, and so do people who are a success at what they do.

▶ *Visualization* is seeing an image in your mind *as if you have already won.* That vision seems real when you think hard about it. Pretty cool, huh?

▶ Visualization can keep you excited and motivated. Do you remember when we read poem number 29, "Staying Motivated"?

▶ What is it you want to be a winner at? Can you picture being that winner in your mind? Let's try it. Think really hard, and try to see it happening right now. Hold onto that image in your mind. What do you see, and what do you feel?

▶ Sometimes winners will even make a Vision Board. Do you want me to help you make a Vision Board for your room?

▶ We can cut out pictures of things that you want to be a winner at and glue them onto the board. We can even glue on pictures of places you would like to visit someday. What do you say? Do you want to make that board?

32. Making Decisions

Sometimes, making decisions is hard to do.
Sometimes, making decisions is easy, too.
Sometimes you're right, and sometimes you're wrong,
but making lots of them can make you strong.
The more you make, the easier it'll be
to make better decisions—just wait and see.
If you need my help, I am always here
to help make the right decision clear.

Engaging Questions to Ask Your Child

► Do you understand why *making decisions* strengthens you? It builds up your confidence.
► Do you know that making even wrong decisions can teach you things? It teaches you what will *not* work. Making *wrong decisions is how we grow and learn*. So don't be afraid to make a decision.
► Are you fearful of making wrong decisions?
► Has there ever been a time when you couldn't decide—or just didn't know what to do? Tell me about it.
► Are there any decisions you need to make now?
► I'm here to help you. You know that, right?

33. Taking Action

If there's something you've decided to get done,
then why haven't you already begun?
Putting things off is a bad habit, it's true.
Is it laziness or fear that is stopping you?
There is even a word for describing it.
Procrastination is the word that fits.

Engaging Questions to Ask Your Child

▸ Do you understand what procrastination is and why it is a bad habit? *Putting things off for a later time is procrastination.* You will never get anything done if you don't have the habit of *taking action.*

▸ Laziness is one reason people procrastinate. You're not lazy, are you? We'll talk more about laziness in poem number 38, "Don't Be Lazy." Okay?

▸ Being fearful is another reason people procrastinate. We'll talk more about being fearful in the next poem, "Not Fearing Failure." Okay?

▸ When your decision seems like a good one, never hesitate to act. All right?

▸ If you are in doubt about your decision to move forward, it's okay to ask me for my opinion first. Okay?

▸ Have you ever wanted to do something but kept putting it off until later? Tell me about it.

34. Not Fearing Failure

Never fear failure. It's a friend to you.
Learning from failure is what you should do.
Each time you fail, just stick out your chin,
and tell yourself with confidence, "I'm going to win.
Failure will not stop me, for I know the truth:
I'm not a failure because of one goof.
Failure may stop me for just this one time,
but I will learn and continue until success becomes mine."

Engaging Questions to Ask Your Child

▶ When was the last time you failed at something? Did you feel hurt or discouraged? Tell me about it.

▶ Do you know that failing is a good thing? *Failing* is your friend—it's *another way we learn.*

▶ Do you fear failure?

▶ Does failing make you want to quit?

▶ You are not a quitter, are you?

▶ Do you remember that you can never win at anything if you keep quitting?

▶ Do you remember that you must never quit trying? I believe in you, and you should believe in yourself. You are not a quitter. Right?

35. Making Mistakes

We all make mistakes, and that is okay.
Mistakes can happen almost any day.
We all *learn something when mistakes are made.*
That's important—so don't be afraid.
If you learn from every mistake,
your next decision will be better—so give yourself a break!

Engaging Questions to Ask Your Child

▶ *All of us make mistakes.* Don't you agree? I know I do.
▶ Do you make mistakes? What mistakes have you made?
▶ Mistakes are okay. We learn from them. If you *learn from your mistakes,* they can be helpful and beneficial. Do you understand?
▶ When we make a mistake, we learn what not to do the next time. It's a learning process. So, there is no reason to feel bad about making a mistake. Do you understand that?

36. Owning Your Mistakes

Never blame others for a mistake you made.
Mistakes can happen, so don't be afraid.
Everyone makes mistakes now and then.
It's not a big deal—it will happen again.
Just remember it takes a humble person to say,
"I made that mistake, but it'll be okay."

Engaging Questions to Ask Your Child

- ▶ You do know that you should always be honest and truthful, right? It's not right to blame others. Have you ever blamed someone else for your mistakes? Explain that to me.
- ▶ You can be proud of yourself for admitting you made a mistake. Do you understand? Always be truthful to yourself and others. Always admit your mistakes. It's called *owning your mistakes*. People will respect you for it when they see that you are truthful.
- ▶ Besides, mistakes are no big deal. Everyone makes them. The main thing is *not to blame someone else*. Right?
- ▶ One other thing about mistakes: always learn from them. Okay?

37. Confronting Your Problems

If you have a problem that bears on your mind,
I'll be there for you, and a solution we'll find.
Problems are common, and their solutions are, too.
We'll solve the problem. I will help you.
So, don't you worry when problems appear.
I'll help you to solve them—so, don't you fear.

Engaging Questions to Ask Your Child

▶ Do you have any problems right now? What are they?
▶ Never hesitate to talk about them. I am here for you. Okay?
▶ Problems are always around. So are the solutions. There is no reason to fear them or get upset. Facing your problems is called *"confronting"* them. Okay?
▶ When *problems* arise, *face them head-on*. You can always ask me for advice. Okay?
▶ Problems make us stronger and smarter. Do you know that? They help us grow and become stronger.

38. Don't Be Lazy

Being lazy is a terrible thing for you.
And people will disrespect you for it, too.
Being lazy won't get anything done,
and, eventually, it'll stop being fun.
Your room will get messy and cluttered as well,
and if you don't clean it, it may start to smell.
Being lazy is not a good trait.
Being lazy . . . well, it's not really that great.
So, never be lazy. Be energetic instead,
and get that laziness out of your head.

Engaging Questions to Ask Your Child

- ▶ You know what *lazy* means, right?
- ▶ Are you lazy about anything? What things are you lazy about? Homework? Keeping your room clean? Picking up the yard?
- ▶ Do you understand that laziness can affect a lot of different things? For example, people could start disrespecting you and could stop trusting you. You may even start losing friends. *Being lazy* is really *a bad habit*. It affects almost everything. Laziness can make you really sad and can make your life very unhappy.

 39. Being Patient

The things that you wish for may not happen today,
but don't get discouraged. They will come your way.
Don't be angry, but be of good cheer.
It may take some time for your wishes to appear.
Being patient is waiting without getting mad.
If you wait with patience, you won't be sad.
Being happy and cheerful is the best way to be.
So, let's wait and be patient. Don't you agree?

Engaging Questions to Ask Your Child

▶ Do you understand what *being patient* is? Let me explain further!
▶ Do you get upset when things don't happen fast enough for you? Do you get discouraged or angry? Has that ever happened to you? Tell me about it.
▶ Do you know that patience makes you stronger?
▶ Do you know that when you have patience, you'll feel happier?

40. Being a Leader

To be a leader, you must really care.
You must care for others and for their welfare.
You can lead by showing how to get things done.
Leading and showing can be lots of fun.
Being a leader can be hard as well.
Do you want to lead? Only you can tell.
To be a leader from the very start,
you must be strong in mind and strong in heart.
But it is *you* who must decide what you want to do.
Is being a leader the right thing for you?

Engaging Questions to Ask Your Child

- ▶ Do you understand now what *being a leader* means? Do you want me to explain it some more?
- ▶ Being a leader means that, first, you must *care for others*. Do you understand?
- ▶ Do you care about the well-being of others?
- ▶ Do you know that, if you learn everything we are reading about, you will make a great leader?
- ▶ Does being a leader interest you? Would you like to be a leader? Why?

41. Making Friends

Making friends is not hard to do,
when you treat others like you want them to treat you.
They will like and respect you the way you respect them
and will stay at your side as incredibly good friends.
So, try to be friendly with everyone each day,
and just watch what happens to you along the way.

Engaging Questions to Ask Your Child

- ▶ Do you want to *make more friends*?
- ▶ Do you understand why respecting others is important? Do you remember when we talked about this in poem number 14, "Respecting Other People"?
- ▶ Do you understand why it is important to treat others like you want to be treated? Remember what we talked about in poem number 18, "Giving and Receiving"? *You must first **give** something in order to **receive** it.*
- ▶ Always show respect for others first. Do you understand?
- ▶ Has this talk helped you to understand how to easily make more friends?

42. Staying Calm

Not everyone will be nice to you,
but stay calm and be patient—whatever they do.
Maybe they're sad or unhappy today.
Maybe some things are not going their way.
So, treat them as nicely as you wish they'd treat you,
and hope that they lose all of their sadness, too.

Engaging Questions to Ask Your Child

- ▶ How do you treat others who are mean to you?
- ▶ When was the last time someone was mean to you? Did you argue with them?
- ▶ Do you remember what we said about arguing?
- ▶ Do you remember that you should treat others like you want them to treat you? When they are not nice to you, maybe they are having a difficult day.
- ▶ Do you remember what we said about respecting others?
- ▶ Do you understand that, when someone is mean, you can still *stay calm*, keep your cool, be nice, and walk away?

43. Forgiving Others

When someone does something to you that is wrong,
you must remember to always stay strong.
Don't let your feelings bring you down,
Don't let your feelings cause you to frown.
Be strong and forgiving in all that you do.
And always remember that forgiveness strengthens you.

Engaging Questions to Ask Your Child

- ▶ Has anyone done something wrong to you recently?
- ▶ How did it make you feel?
- ▶ Do you know that, when you are able to *forgive someone*, it makes you feel good about your-self? It makes you stronger inside.
- ▶ Have you ever forgiven anyone? Tell me about it. How did forgiving them make you feel?
- ▶ When someone does something wrong to you, you should remember not to let it bring you down. Okay? *Stay strong, and forgive* that person. Remember that you can always talk to me.
- ▶ Forgiveness is an excellent quality. When you can forgive, it makes you stronger. Do you understand?

44. Having Good Manners

Having good manners will make you look good.
Be kind and considerate. Is that understood?
When you show good manners, you'll feel good inside,
and you will like yourself for knowing you tried.
Be polite in your actions, and you will find
that people will like you most of the time.
Be polite around others, show them your best,
and then watch what happens—you will be blessed.

Engaging Questions to Ask Your Child

▸ Here are a few examples of *bad manners: burping aloud, playing with your food, picking your nose, interrupting someone while they are speaking, yelling, being disrespectful, and talking back.* Can you think of more?

▸ Do you know that most people will like you and respect you if you are polite and *have good manners*?

▸ Do you want people to respect you? Remember us talking about respect?

▸ Do you know that when you are polite and show good manners, it makes you feel better about yourself?

▸ If you feel better about yourself, it makes you happier, more confident, and stronger. Do you remember poem number 5, "Liking Yourself"?

▸ It's important to like yourself and feel good inside—right? How does *having good manners* and being polite to someone make you feel inside?

45. Cleanliness

A bath should be taken once every day.
A bath should be taken to keep the germs away.
When I say it's time to go get clean,
you shouldn't think that I'm being mean.
I want you to be healthy and to be strong.
Besides, taking a bath shouldn't take that long.
Also remember that, before each meal,
washing your hands is a big, big deal.
Remember to wash your hands after you play,
because that, too, helps keep those nasty germs away.

Engaging Questions to Ask Your Child

- ▶ Do you understand the importance of *cleanliness*?
- ▶ You want to stay healthy and strong, don't you?
- ▶ You don't want those nasty germs crawling all over you, do you?
- ▶ Germs are too small to see. It takes a microscope to see them. Have you ever seen pictures of those nasty germs? They are ugly things that we need to wash away. Do you want to see some pictures of germs?
- ▶ Do you know that staying clean will help keep away a lot of sickness caused by those nasty germs?
- ▶ After a bath, we always feel good, don't we?

46. Brushing Your Teeth

Brushing your teeth after you chew
should be one of the things most important to you.
By brushing your teeth after each meal,
your smiles will be sparkling—and that's a big deal.
So, remember to brush your teeth every day.
Then you won't have to worry about tooth decay.

Engaging Questions to Ask Your Child

- ▶ Do you brush your teeth every day?
- ▶ Have you ever had pain from tooth decay? It really hurts.
- ▶ Do you know that *brushing your teeth* will kill those nasty germs that cause tooth decay?
- ▶ Do you know that keeping your teeth clean—and gums, too—is a very important thing to do? It keeps those nasty germs that cause tooth decay out of your mouth!
- ▶ What do you think about those nasty germs?

 47. Eating Healthy

Eating candy is a fun thing to do.
But eating too much is not good for you.
Instead, choose foods that are healthy and nutritious.
Many of them will be very delicious.
Apples, pears, and grapes can be fun and healthy to eat,
and so are veggies, grains, dairy, and meat.
But remember what I am telling you today:
Eating too much candy is not the way.
It's not the way to stay healthy and strong.
So, eat less of it , and you won't be wrong.

Engaging Questions to Ask Your Child

▶ Do you know that, to stay healthy, you must *eat healthy food*? Do you know that vegetables are super important—even spinach?

▶ What kinds of foods do you think are healthy? Let's talk about it.

▶ What kinds of healthy foods do you like?

▶ Candy is fun to eat. But did you know that too much isn't healthy? Too much can make you sick. I bet you didn't know that, huh?

▶ Too much candy can also cause tooth decay. Tooth decay hurts, right? Those tooth-decay germs love candy a lot.

48. Fresh Air and Exercise

Fresh air and exercise are good for you,
and playing outdoors can be fun to do.
If going outdoors with a friend to play
is something you want to do today,
then call your friend, and ask them to
come over to your yard to play with you.
If you would rather go to their home,
then, first, you must call them on the phone.
If there's a reason you can't go, that's okay.
You and I can stay home and play.

Engaging Questions to Ask Your Child

▸ Do you know that *fresh air, sunlight, and exercise* are healthy and good for you? They help you to grow up strong and healthy.
▸ Do you like playing outdoors with your friends?
▸ What kinds of games do you play outdoors? Tell me.
▸ Do you want to go out and play?

49. Getting Plenty of Rest

Getting plenty of rest is good for you,
whether you take a nap or sleep the night through.
Getting lots of sleep is healthy, you know.
Getting lots of sleep will help you grow.
When you hear me say it's time to lie down,
You shouldn't get upset, and you shouldn't frown.
Do you know that I want what's best for you?
So, listen to me, whatever you do.

Engaging Questions to Ask Your Child

- Do you know that *plenty of sleep and rest* is healthy for you? It will help you to grow and be strong.
- You want to grow strong and healthy, don't you?
- Do you know that taking a nap during the day is also healthy? Your body needs time to rest and grow stronger.
- When you lie down to rest, what do you think about?
- Do you want me to read to you when you lie down? *(optional)*
- Do you enjoy me reading to you at bedtime? You know that reading and listening are important, right? *(optional)*

50. When You Grow Up

When you grow up, what would you like to be?
A doctor, or a lawyer, or the owner of a company?
Growing up will be exciting, and I am curious to know:
Where would you like to travel? Where would you like to go?
The world is full of wonders, and it's my hope that you'll see
its bountiful treasures, its beauty and majesty.

Engaging Questions to Ask Your Child

- ▶ Have you ever thought about *what you want to be when you grow up*?
- ▶ Have you ever thought about *where you want to visit or live when you grow up*?
- ▶ It's fun thinking about these things, huh? Just remember that you can do anything and go anywhere if you really believe it. You and I can put these things on your Vision Board and Goal Board if you want.
- ▶ What things would you like to put on your Vision Board and your Goal Board?

About the Author

The author grew up in an impoverished family of seven children in a small rural town in Illinois. He didn't have much growing up, but he had a mother who encouraged him to excel. During his early childhood, his mother instilled in him a belief that he was extraordinarily gifted.

After graduating high school and a successful stint in the U.S. Navy, he went on to earn a Bachelor of Science Degree in Business Administration with a Specialization in Marketing. He graduated in the top ten percent of his class and was on his college's Dean's List and the National Dean's List.

After college, he went on to experience forty years of success in sales. During his career, he won more than a dozen production awards. At one point, he was one of the two top producers for an international company that employed several hundred independent contractors. Twelve of those forty years were spent working with a publisher of children's books.

He attributes his success to a much higher authority, to his mother, who planted the seeds for his success early in life, to his drive to succeed, and to all the self-improvement books that he has faithfully read.

Request for Reviews

Thank you for taking the time to share this book with your child.
We sincerely hope the contents of this book will help your child
grow strong in character and to reach his or her potential.

Like all authors, I rely on online reviews to encourage future sales.
Your opinion is invaluable. Would you take a few moments now to share
your assessment of my book at a review site of your choice.
Your opinion will help the book to reach more families like yours.